Bees and Wasps

James Maclaine

Designed by Will Dawes, Sam Chandler and Alice Reese

Illustrated by John Francis and Kimberley Scott

Bee and wasp consultant: Chris O'Toole FRES,
Honorary Research Associate, Oxford University Museum of Natural History

Reading consultant: Alison Kelly, Principal Lecturer at the University of Roehampton

Contents

Hairy insects

Bees and wasps are types of insects. Wasps have thin, smooth bodies and legs, but bees are fatter and furrier.

This is a bumblebee.

It has lots of fuzzy hairs on its legs and body that keep it warm.

Body parts

Bees and wasps have some parts of their bodies that are the same.

All bees and wasps have six legs. At the end of each leg is a tiny claw that's good for gripping.

They have two feelers on their heads that they use to smell and touch.

Most bees and wasps have two pairs of wings. One pair of wings is smaller than the other.

This photograph shows a type of large wasp called a hornet.

Not all bees and wasps are black and yellow. Some have brown, red, blue or green bodies.

Fast fliers

Most bees and wasps can fly.

Before a bee flies it warms itself by resting in the sun or shaking its body.

If a bumblebee gets wet, it can't fly. It has to wait until it's dry again.

Some wasps can't fly at all.

Female velvet ant wasps, like this one, don't have any wings.

The buzzing sound you hear from a bee or wasp is made when it flaps its wings.

Bumblebees have big, round bodies but their wings are small. They have to beat their wings very quickly so they can fly.

This is a red-tailed bumblebee.

It beats its wings 200 times every second to stay in the air.

Living together

Solitary bees and wasps live alone. Other types of bees and wasps live together in groups called colonies.

A colony of Asian dwarf honey bees lives in this nest.

There are many honey bees in each colony.

Most of the bees are workers. They're all female. The workers take care of the nest.

A few of the bees are male. They have large eyes and are known as drones.

The biggest bee is the queen. She's the mother of every bee in the colony.

A queen makes smells to tell things to the bees in her nest.

Workers

The worker bees or wasps in a colony do lots of different jobs.

Some workers take care of the queen. They feed and clean her.

These worker honey bees are cleaning the queen's body with their front legs.

Workers mend holes in the nest. They make it bigger, too.

They keep the nest safe by guarding the entrance.

If the nest gets hot, they fan in cool air with their wings.

When it's cold, they huddle together to warm up the nest.

Builders

Different bees and wasps build different types of nests.

This queen wasp is building a nest from paper. She makes the paper by chewing wood.

The nest is made up of lots of cells. Each cell has six sides.

Solitary bees and wasps make small nests.

A leafcutter bee
places pieces of leaf
inside a hole to
make a nest.

A potter wasp builds
nests from mud.
Each nest looks like
a small pot.

A carpenter bee
makes a nest by
chewing a long
tunnel into wood.

Some bumblebees line their
nests with moss.

Laying eggs

In a colony, it's a queen's job to lay eggs.

This paper wasp is a queen.
She's laying an egg in one
of the cells in her nest.

A queen honey bee can lay more
than a thousand eggs in a day.

All female solitary bees and wasps lay eggs in their nests. They also put some food in the nests for their young to eat.

A tarantula hawk wasp finds a spider and stings it so that it can't move.

Then, the wasp drags the spider back to her nest in the ground.

She lays an egg in the nest. When it hatches, the young wasp eats the spider.

Hatching out

As bees and wasps grow up, their bodies change a lot.

A baby honey bee or larva hatches out of its egg.

Worker bees feed the larva while it grows in its cell.

After a week, the workers cover the larva's cell with wax.

Inside, it slowly changes shape. It's now called a pupa.

Over two weeks, the pupa changes into an adult. First, its eyes turn hard and black. Then, its skin becomes harder, too.

Wasps grow in a similar way. This paper wasp has changed into an adult. It's using its jaws to break out of its cell.

Finding food

Bees and wasps spend a lot of their time looking for food.

They visit flowers to drink a sweet juice called nectar.

They also eat sap, a juice that oozes from broken branches.

Bees eat pollen, too. Pollen is a yellow powder made by flowers.

This bumblebee is putting pollen onto its back leg, to carry to its nest.

Wasps eat other types of sweet food. These wasps are eating a plum.

They're fighting each other to get near it.

If wasps eat too much ripe fruit, they become sleepy.

Making seeds

Many bees and some wasps help flowering plants to make seeds.

Bees have to visit lots of flowers to find the food they need.

1. Each time a bee lands on a flower, pollen sticks to the hairs on its body.

2. The bee flies to another flower of the same kind. Some pollen brushes off the bee.

3. The pollen helps the plant make seeds. These then grow into new plants.

Some bees visit more than two thousand flowers each day.

On guard

Bees and wasps protect themselves and the places where they live.

Male wool carder bees chase away insects that come to the flowers they feed on.

Honey bees make a ball around a hornet that enters their nest.

Wasps scare away other insects by standing on their back legs.

Most bees and wasps also protect themselves by stinging. They sting with a pointed tube that injects poison.

You can see the tube at the end of this yellow paper wasp's body.

Female bees and wasps can sting, but males can't.

Sending messages

Bees and wasps tell each other things by moving their bodies and making smells.

This buff-tailed bumblebee is feeding on lavender flowers.

It leaves a smell on the flowers so other bees from its nest can find them.

If a honey bee finds some flowers, it flies back to the nest to tell the other bees.

The bee moves in a pattern that shows the others where the flowers are.

Then, the other bees leave the nest and go to find the flowers, too.

When a wasp or bee stings someone, it makes a smell. This warns the colony of danger.

Honey makers

Worker honey bees make honey as food for their colony.

Bees suck up nectar from flowers and turn it into honey in their tummies.

The bees carry the honey back to their nest and spit it into cells.

Then, other worker bees fan the honey with their wings. This makes it thicker.

Wasps can't make honey, but they do steal it from bees' nests.

People keep bees for their honey. They make boxes known as hives for the honey bees to live in.

These bees are flying back to a hive. Their nest is inside the hive.

New nests

Most colonies of bees and wasps die before winter, but the queens survive.

A queen bumblebee goes to sleep in a hole in the ground for winter.

In spring, the queen wakes up and crawls out of her resting place.

Then, she starts to build a new nest. She lays eggs in pots she makes from wax.

When a honey
bee nest gets too
crowded, the
queen flies away.

Some bees from
her colony follow
her in a group
called a swarm.

This swarm is looking for
a place to build a new nest.

Glossary

Here are some of the words in this book you might not know. This page tells you what they mean.

 colony - a group of bees or wasps living together.

 worker - a female bee or wasp that does different jobs for a colony.

 queen - the biggest bee or wasp in a colony. A queen lays eggs.

 larva - a baby bee or wasp. Each larva hatches out of an egg.

 pupa - a bee or wasp that's slowly changing into an adult.

 nectar - a sweet juice made by flowers. Bees and wasps eat nectar.

 pollen - a yellow powder that bees eat. Pollen is made by flowers.

Websites to visit

You can visit exciting websites to find out more about bees and wasps.

To visit these websites, go to the Usborne Quicklinks Website at **www.usborne.com/quicklinks** Read the internet safety guidelines, and then type the keywords "**beginners bees**".

The websites are regularly reviewed and the links in Usborne Quicklinks are updated. However, Usborne Publishing is not responsible, and does not accept liability, for the content or availability of any website other than its own. We recommend that children are supervised while on the internet.

This common wasp is drinking water while resting on a leaf.

Index

Acknowledgements

Photographic manipulation by Mike Olley
Cover design by Zoe Wray

Photo credits
The publishers are grateful to the following for permission to reproduce material:
cover © **Jonn/Johnér Images/Corbis**; p1© **Patrick Pleul/dpa/Corbis**; p2-3 © **Geoff du Feu/ardea.com**;
p4-5 © **Michael Durham/Minden Pictures/Corbis**; p6 © **James Carmichael Jr/NHPA/Photoshot**;
p7 © **ImageBroker/Imagebroker/FLPA**; p8 © **imagebroker.net/SuperStock**; p10-11 © **Visuals Unlimited,
Inc./Eric Tourneret/Getty Images**; p12 © **John Mason/ardea.com**; p14 © **John Cancalosi/ardea.com**; p17
© **Ken Wilson; Papilio/CORBIS**; p18 © **Ken Preston-Mafham/Premaphotos Wildlife**; p19 © **Brian Bevan/
ardea.com**; p23 © **Olivier Parent/Alamy**; p24 © **Peter O'Toole**; p27 © **Mike Powles/Getty Images**; p29
© **Heidi & Hans-Juergen Koch/Minden Pictures/FLPA**; p31 © **Steve Downer/ardea.com**

Every effort has been made to trace and acknowledge ownership of copyright. If any rights have
been omitted, the publishers offer to rectify this in any subsequent editions following notification.